RANK AND RATE

VOLUME II: INSIGNIA OF ROYAL NAVAL RATINGS, WRNS, ROYAL MARINES, QARNNS AND AUXILIARIES

E.C. COLEMAN

The Crowood Press

First published in 2011 by
The Crowood Press Ltd
Ramsbury, Marlborough
Wiltshire SN8 2HR

www.crowood.com

British Library Cataloguing-in-Publication Data
A catalogue record for this book is available from
the British Library.

ISBN 978 1 84797 308 5

Printed and bound in China by Everbest Printing Co. Ltd

Contents

1 Introduction

Before the middle years of the eighteenth century, naval dress was considered to be a matter whose interest did not reach much further than that of the wearer himself. However, in 1748, after respectful prompting by naval officers, the Admiralty ordered that those officers should wear a uniform pattern of dress. The uniformity was not to come from distinguishing decoration such as badges or stripes. Instead, Admirals were to wear one style of uniform, Captains another, Lieutenants another, and so on. It was to be over a century before the formal means of distinguishing between the ranks of naval officers took on the form recognizable today.

Naval ratings (those below the rank of commissioned officer) found events happening in the reverse order. A badge was introduced for Petty Officers in 1827 and more badges arrived in 1853, with the creation of Chief Petty Officers and Leading

A 1950s poster showing the regulations regarding the correct positioning of badges.

Hands. Yet it was to be another four years before Admiralty Circular No. 283 was promulgated, ordering the wearing of a uniform by all naval ratings.

The Royal Marines, by virtue of their military background, have worn military-style rank insignia since their original formation. As with all branches of the Royal Navy, crowns on badges have changed as sovereigns have arrived and departed, and new designs have imposed change, but the basic stars ('pips') and stripes have remained as the basis for Royal Marine insignia.

With the introduction, however, of women as nursing sisters at the end of the nineteenth century, a new form of distinction was needed as the basis for a code of discipline on the hospital wards. Queen Alexandra's Naval Nursing Service amply demonstrated the importance of its role in progressing from acting as assistants to the surgeons to becoming fully fledged naval officers within a century. The nurses, despite their late introduction into the Service, took less than fifty years to rank on an equal footing with Royal Naval ratings.

In a similar recognition of ability, the Women's Royal Naval Service, after being disbanded within two years of its foundation in the First World War, re-emerged as a vital component of the Royal Navy's work, in both war and peace, at the outbreak of the Second World War. Taken into the Royal Navy towards the end of the twentieth century as equal members of the Service, the WRNS sadly lost not only their honoured name, but also the traditional 'blue for a girl' distinguishing insignia. The Royal Navy's auxiliaries seem always to be at the mercy of Treasury cuts. Manned by volunteers, they are the easiest target, and difficult to defend when the only option remaining was to cut the Royal Navy itself. Their unique insignia is included as a memorial to those who put country before self.

The Royal Fleet Auxiliary is included for the obvious reason that, without them, the support and supply of the Royal Navy's ships on operations would be drastically, and adversely, affected.

Unusually, in such a volume, the basic, official Merchant Navy insignia is included. The work done by the British mercantile marine, in both peace and war, cannot be over-estimated, and it has earned its place alongside the branches of the Royal Navy.

Rating's Badge

The first badges for ratings in the Royal Navy were those promulgated by an Admiralty Circular in June 1827. These early badges were cut from white material for use against a dark background. Later, when white clothing came into use, blue badges on a white background were introduced. The first gold-plated wire badges appeared on best ('Number 1') uniforms in 1853 and, in 1860, the white on blue badges were replaced by red on blue for Number 2 uniforms. (Ratings serving in the Royal Yacht continued to wear white on blue badges on their Number

2 uniforms until there was no longer a Royal Yacht in which to serve.) The rate badge appearance and design remained basically unchanged until the end of the twentieth century, when the elegant gold-wire badges were phased out and replaced by a shiny, man-made, gold-coloured thread. The red on black badges disappeared along with the No.2 uniform in 1994.

Whilst the message inherent within each rate badge is linked firmly to the wearer's rate, the same inflexibility cannot be applied to the design and dimensions of the badges themselves. Even in an age of dull uniformity, although sealed patterns exist as they always have, slight variations have constantly, albeit inadvertently, arisen due to changes in manufacturer -- of which there have been many. It is also necessary to be aware that the wearing of obsolete badges is (and was) a common occurrence within the Royal Navy. Changes in the design of the crown, for example, St Edward's to Tudor in 1901, and the reverse in 1953, did not mean a wholesale change of badges. Both officers and ratings could be found still wearing the Tudor crown in the early 1960s and, in one extreme case, the last Sailmaker in the Royal Navy retired in 1986 still wearing a Tudor crown on his working 'rig'. The simple reason for this was the fact that his branch, very small in numbers, had not used up all its old stock before re-ordering became necessary.

One small alteration that can assist in generally dating badges that incorporate a crown came about shortly after the First World War. At that time, the centre jewel in the front of the crown was changed from red to blue. Again, no strict dating can be applied as several years were to pass before all the old stocks were exhausted.

It is odd to reflect that a man who had served with Nelson and lived to a modest age would have no difficulty in recognizing the rate of today's men and women serving in the Royal Navy's 'lower deck'. A modern, nuclear-age rating could be wearing a badge that might have been seen on the arm of an early nineteenth-century Petty Officer. It is not, however, the badge that makes the individual, but the tradition behind it.

Contemporary drawing of a 1st Class Petty Officer wearing his 1827 issue badge.

The original 1827 Admiralty Circular that recognised the status of Petty Officers with the introduction of rate badges.

2 Post-1970 Warrant Officers' Cuffs

When Warrant Officers were re-introduced to the Royal Navy, in 1970, they were given a rate that made them equal to the Army's Warrant Officer 1st Class. It inevitably followed, therefore, that they would be given the same badge: the Royal Coat of Arms, complete with crest, supporters and motto. This design, also following Army tradition, was known as the 'Tate and Lyle' badge after the design on the popular tin of treacle. They were also given the official title of Fleet Chief Petty Officer in place of requests to be known as 'Master Chief', or even 'Super Chief'. In 1990, a smaller version of the cuff badge was introduced for wear with mess dress.

Again, in accordance with military custom, the Warrant Officer 2nd Class was introduced in 2004 complete with a new cuff badge.

Fleet Chief Petty Officer (left cuff) 1971–1973.

Fleet Chief Petty Officer 1973–1985 (left cuff). Warrant Officer 1985–2004 (both cuffs). Warrant Officer 1st Class 2004–.

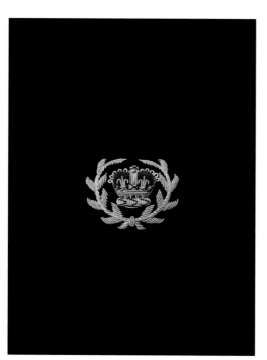

Warrant Officer 2nd Class 2004–.

3 Post-1970 Warrant Officers' Cap Badges

The introduction of military-style Warrant Officers under the title of Fleet Chief Petty Officers led to the requirement for a new cap badge. The design chosen was a more elaborate version of the Chief Petty Officer's cap badge. In practice, this was eventually seen as unsuccessful and, in 1990, a new design was introduced, which brought the cap badge closer in appearance to the Officer's cap badge.

Fleet Chief Petty Officer 1970–1985. Warrant Officer 1985–1990.

Metal beret badge, Fleet Chief Petty Officer 1970–1985. Warrant Officer 1985–1990.

Warrant Officer 1990–2004. Warrant Officer 1st and 2nd Class 2004–.

Warrant Officer 1st and 2nd Class.

Metal beret badge, Warrant Officer 1990–2004. Warrant Officer 1st and 2nd Class 2004.

4 Chief Petty Officers' Rate Badges 1857–

The rating of Chief Petty Officer first appeared in the Royal Navy in 1853, an event marked by the issue of a special badge to indicate the wearer's rate. The badge was modified (with laurel leaves replacing oak leaves) with the issue of the first official uniforms in 1857. The uniforms for Chief Petty Officers remained as the 'square rig' worn by all ratings until 1879 when they were put into the long jacket and peaked cap 'fore and aft rig' of Schoolmasters, Engine Room Artificers and others. They continued, nevertheless, to wear their arm badge until it was withdrawn in 1890. For the next thirty years, the rate insignia for Chief Petty Officers was limited to his cap badge, his branch badges on his jacket lapels, and his buttons. The next Chief Petty Officer's rate badge to be worn on the arm was that worn by Chief Petty Officers fighting alongside the army as part of the Royal Naval Division – sailors of the Royal Navy who served in infantry battalions between 1914 and 1919.

Cuff buttons were awarded to all Chief Petty Officers in 1920, thus continuing a dress feature that had begun with the buttons that held up the 'boot' cuffs of the original naval officer's uniform of 1748. The change in the various artificer branches from their rates of 4th to 1st Class being replaced with Leading Hand to Chief Petty Officer titles, was seen as diminishing the standing of the most senior artificer, the Chief Artificer. To counteract this loss of standing, the rating of Charge Chief Artificer was introduced in the early 1980s. They were given a cuff badge with the incongruous – certainly non-naval – image of a rampant lion before being replaced by the Warrant Officer 2nd Class.

Pre-official uniform

1853–1857. Worn on upper left sleeve in best clothing.

1853–1857. Worn with working clothing.

1853–1857. For wear with white clothing.

On the introduction of an official uniform in 1857 (worn on upper left arm)

1857–1890. 'No. 1' uniform.

1857–1860. 'No. 2' uniform.

1860–1890. 'No. 2' uniform.

1857–1890. For wear with white uniform.

Chief Petty Officer c.1880.

Chief Petty Officer Royal
Naval Division 1914–1919 (right cuff).

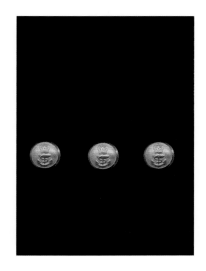

All Chief Petty Officers, 1920, both cuffs.
(Queen's crown from 1953.)

Chief Petty Officer Pilot 1912–1948
(left cuff).

Chief Petty Officer Observer 1912–1948
(left cuff).

Chief Petty Officer Observer No. 2
uniform (left cuff).

Chief Petty Officer
Aircrewman (U) (left cuff).

Chief Petty Officer Pilot tropical uniform (left cuff).

Chief Petty Officer Observer tropical uniform (left cuff).

Charge Chief Artificer, right cuff (replaced by Warrant Officer 2nd Class in 2004).

Charge Chief Artificer, right cuff (on No. 2 uniform until 1995).

Charge Chief Artificer, right cuff, tropical uniform.

Early (laurel leaf) version of Chief Petty Officer's badge 1857–1860.

Chief Petty Officer c.1880.

Chief Petty Officer Royal Naval Division 1915.

5 Chief Petty Officers' Cap Badges, Military Branch, 1879–1920

Military branch Chief Petty Officers came from the seaman and signalling branches. They wore cap badges with gold and silver embroidery and silver anchors in exactly the same manner as officers from the same branches wore theirs. In the case of the Chief Petty Officers of the Royal Naval Division, bronze badges were introduced for wear on the Western Front.

1879–1901.

1879–1901 variant.

Original 1901 pattern.

1901–1920. Central jewel changed to blue in 1920.

Metal sun helmet badge 1901–1920.

Bronze for wear ashore with khaki uniform 1914–1920.

c.1895.

c.1895.

6 Chief Petty Officers' Cap Badges, Civil Branch, 1879–1920

The civil branches of the Royal Navy were made up of all branches other than the seamen and the signallers (the Engine Room Artificers, however, are not included here as they had particular variations to their cap badges). The cap badges of the civil branch Chief Petty Officers followed the same design principles as the civil branch officers with gold anchors, and with all gold thread used in the embroidery. Civil branch Chief Petty Officers serving ashore with the Royal Naval Division wore the same bronze badge as the military branch. The brass and silver metal badge worn by the military branch was also worn by civil branch Chief Petty Officers when wearing the sun helmet.

1879–1901.

1879–1901 variant.

Original 1901 pattern.

1901–1920.

c.1890.

7 Chief Petty Officers' Cap Badges, All Branches, 1920–

With the introduction in 1920 of 'fore and aft rig' for all military branch Petty Officers of four years' seniority (civil branch Petty Officers had been wearing the uniform since 1890, but with a red embroidered cap badge), it was decided that Petty Officers should have a dedicated cap badge. This, in turn, meant that Chief Petty Officers required a cap badge of a distinguishing, new design. All the basic elements of the previous badge – crown, anchor, and rope circle – were retained, now to be accompanied by a wreath of laurel leaves surrounding the anchor. In addition, with the officers abandoning the gold/silver anchor cap badge variations between the military and the civil branches in 1918, Chief Petty Officers followed the same direction. During the Second World War, both all-metal and utility versions were produced.

1920–1953.

1920 pattern variant.

All metal sun helmet badge 1920–1939.
Beret badge 1939–1953.

Metal variety on cloth
1939–1945.

Flat wartime economy version
1939–1945.

1953–.

Metal beret badge 1953–.

c.1920.

c.1920.

c.2007.

8 Petty Officers, 1853–

Before 1827, the Royal Navy's 'lower deck' consisted of just Able Seamen (including those training to be Able Seamen) and Petty Officers. In that year, it was decided that the duties of Petty Officers had become sufficiently wide and varied to allow for two classes of Petty Officer. To distinguish between the two, a badge for each class of Petty Officer was introduced for wear on the upper left sleeve. The 1st Class Petty Officer was granted an anchor surmounted by a crown, the 2nd Class an anchor. In 1853, with the introduction of the Chief Petty Officer rate, the crown and anchor badge was given to the 2nd Class Petty Officer, whilst a new badge consisting of two crossed anchors beneath a crown was granted to the 1st Class Petty Officer. The rate of 2nd Class Petty Officer was abolished in 1913.

1st Class Petty Officer 1853–1901.

1st Class Petty Officer. For wear with No. 2 uniform 1853–1860 (white thread).

1st Class Petty Officer. For wear with No. 2 uniform 1860–1901 (red thread).

2nd Class Petty Officer 1853–1901.

2nd Class Petty Officer for wear with No. 2 uniform 1853–1860.

2nd Class Petty Officer for wear with No. 2 uniform 1860–1901.

1st Class Petty Officer 1901–1920.

1st Class Petty Officer for wear with No. 2 uniform 1901–1953.

2nd Class Petty Officer 1901–1913. Rate then abolished.

2nd Class Petty Officer for wear with No. 2 uniform 1901–1913.

Petty Officer serving ashore with the Royal Naval Division 1914–1919.

Petty Officer serving ashore and wearing khaki (other than the Royal Naval Division) 1914–1919.

Petty Officer for wear with tropical uniform 1901–1953 (embroidered).

Petty Officer for wear with working uniform 1901–1953 (printed).

Petty Officer 1920–1953 (the blue jewel in the crown replaced the red in 1920).

Petty Officer 1953–.

Petty Officer 1953–1994 (allowed to be worn until 1996).

Petty Officer for wear on working uniform 1953–1995 (printed).

Petty Officer for wear on tropical uniform 1953– (embroidered), working uniform 1995–.

Petty Officer serving in the Royal Yacht 1953–1997. (All badges worn by Royal Yachtsmen were made of white thread.)

Petty Officer wearing camouflage uniform 1991–.

Seaman Gunner Torpedo Man with the rate of Petty Officer 2nd Class c.1885.

A 2nd Class Petty Officer stands in front of a 1st Class Petty Officer c.1895.

Petty Officers c.1895.

Petty Officer c.1895.

Stoker Petty Officer c.1910.

A Petty Officer Seaman Torpedo Man attached to the Naval Wing of the Royal Flying Corps c.1913.

A Petty Officer of the Royal Naval Air Service Armoured Car Division, c.1915. The collar (sometimes lapel) badges are frequently mistaken for cap badges.

Petty Officer in 'No. 8' working dress, 31 July 1970. The date can be ascertained from the fact that he is drinking the last routine issue of a tot of rum on the day it was abolished.

9 Royal Navy Petty Officers' Cap Badges, 1890–

With the introduction in 1890 of the Class III 'fore and aft rig' for all ratings in the civil branches of the Royal Navy, it was decided that those men who held the rate of Petty Officer and below should wear a cap badge. Consequently, they were granted a red thread version of the Chief Petty Officer's cap badge (although one variant had a chain anchor cable in place of the usual rope cable version). The only change to this policy occurred in 1901 with the introduction of the sun helmet. The Petty Officer's metal helmet badge remained with the red colour, whilst the junior ratings wore blue. In 1920, Petty Officers of the military branches of over four years' seniority were authorized to wear the long jacket and peaked cap worn by Chief Petty Officers. As a result, all Petty Officers not wearing the Class II 'square rig' now wore the senior rating's Class I uniform. This, it was felt, deserved a cap badge of its own. Accordingly, as the Chief Petty Officers were granted a cap badge of new design, their old cap badge was passed to the Petty Officers. During the Second World War, both metal and utility thread versions were issued.

Class III uniform 1890–1901. This example shows a chain anchor cable; rope anchor cables were also used in some versions.

Class III uniform 1901–1920.

Class III uniform metal sun helmet badge 1901–1920.

Class I uniform 1920–1953.

Class I metal sun helmet badge 1920–1939. Class I metal beret badge 1939–1953.

All metal badge on cloth Class I 1939–1945.

Flat wartime economy version 1939–1945.

Class I uniform 1953–1966. All Petty Officers 1966–.

Metal beret badge Class I uniform 1953–1966. All Petty Officers 1966–.

Petty Officer in Class III uniform (red embroidered cap badge c.1912.

c.1935.

c.1974.

10 Leading Hands, 1853–

With the introduction of continuous service in 1853, it was decided that there needed to be a rate between Able Seaman and Petty Officer. As a result, the new rate of Leading Hand was brought in to the Royal Navy. The name came from the experienced seaman who led other men out on a ship's yard where they would handle the sails. The distinguishing badge they were granted was the anchor previously worn by 2nd Class Petty Officers. The image gave rise to their nickname of 'Hookys' or 'Hooks', and to their often being referred to as 'Killicks', from an old name for the anchor.

1853. No. 1 dress

1853–1860. Worn by Leading Hands serving in the Royal Yacht until 1997.

1860–1994 (allowed to be worn until 1996).

Printed for working dress until 1995. Embroidered for tropical dress (working dress from 1995).

Leading Hands serving ashore in khaki (other than with the Royal Naval Division) 1914–1919.

Leading Hands serving ashore with the Royal Naval Division 1914–1919.

For wear with camouflage dress 1991–.

Leading Hand c.1895.

Leading Hand c.1942. He is wearing a 'Marksman' badge on his right cuff. The wearing of his cap in a 'flat-a-back' later became frowned upon.

Leading Hand in Class III uniform C.1912.

A Royal Naval Commando Leading Hand, 1943.

Leading Hand serving ashore, c.1916.

c.1905.

c.1916.

Class III uniform (miscellaneous)
1890–1901 (anchor chain version;
anchor rope varieties were also produced).

Class III uniform (Miscellaneous)
Boy Apprentice 1903–1920.
Artificer Apprentice 1920–1953.

Class III (Miscellaneous) metal
sun helmet badge 1901–1920.

Class III (Miscellaneous)
1953–1960. Artificer Apprentice
1953–1997.

Metal beret badge 1976–.

c.1988.

12 Engine Room Artificers, 1868–1918

With the introduction of steam propulsion into the Royal Navy, it was discovered that a better-educated and more technically trained rating was needed. In answer to this requirement, a new branch of the Service was formed, named Engine Room Artificers (ERAs). These were men who had already done their engineering apprenticeships in civilian life and could be employed immediately on entering the Service. They were not 'rated' as normal ratings, but 'classed' according to their experience within the Service. On entering, they were known as 'Acting Engine Room Artificers'; with over three years' service they were classed as '4th Class'; up to seven years, they were '3rd Class'; those with over seven years' service, but fewer than twelve, were '2nd Class'; those with over twelve years' service were '1st Class'. In addition, there were two classes of Chief Engine Room Artificer.

1879–1901.

1901–1918 (then as for Military Branch Chief Petty Officers).

Early variation of the 1901 pattern.

A group of three Engine Room Artificers c.1910.

Engine Room Artificer c.1895.

Engine Room Artificer c.1901.
The spotted tie is unauthorized.

13 Royal Naval Band Service, 1901–1906

During the latter part of the nineteenth century, most sea-going bands of the Royal Navy were made up from Maltese and Italian musicians. In 1874, however, the Service began to see the appearance of band boys who had served in bands on board the Royal Navy's training ships. They were given a uniform consisting of a blue tunic and trousers with a 'pillbox' hat. The tunic was edged with white cord and given a white 'stand-up' collar. The trousers were decorated with two narrow bands of white braid down the outer seams, and the hat bore a band of black braid trimmed with white. Bandmasters wore silver braid on the trousers and the hat, whilst their tunic

was trimmed with black braid and had a black collar. A cap badge was introduced in 1901. Unfortunately, according to a report of 1902, 'The appearance, system of training, and standard of efficiency of Naval bandsmen are unsatisfactory.' This resulted, the following year, in the creation of the Royal Naval School of Music and the formation of the Royal Marines Band Service. The Naval bandsmen were given until 1906 to transfer to the Royal Marines Band Service, or were discharged. Oddly enough, however, the Royal Naval Band Service cap badge continued to appear in the uniform regulations for several more decades.

(Silver thread) Chief Bandmaster, Bandmaster 1901–1906.
(White thread) Band Corporal, Bandsman, Band boy
1901–1906, Musician 1901–1906.

14 Royal Naval Division Petty Officers and Junior Ratings, 1914–1919

In 1914, the number of Royal Naval reservists who mobilized for service on board ships proved to be more than was required. Instead of sending them home, the First Lord of the Admiralty, Winston Churchill, organized them into an infantry division along Army lines. In the beginning, the Royal Naval Division (RND) consisted of three Brigades, two made up of four naval battalions (each named after a famous admiral) and one Royal Marine Brigade. Sent immediately to serve in the defence of Antwerp, the sailors found themselves in trenches wearing seaman's collars and bell-bottomed trousers. Although they did well in the circumstances, several hundred men of the RND were captured by the enemy, whilst others were interred in neutral Holland.

The Division was then sent to Gallipoli where its casualty rate caused the Naval Brigades of the Division to be reduced to three battalions each, with the Collingwood and Benbow battalions being disbanded. Sent to the Western Front in 1916 as the 63rd

(RN) Division, and strengthened by the support of army battalions, they were supplied with full military kit and given battalion cap badges that reflected their eponymous admirals. A machine-gun section was attached and given its own cap badge. As well as being named after admirals, the battalions were also numbered after the Army fashion, and small brass numbers were supplied to wear over the battalion shoulder titles. However, these were almost universally ignored.

The RND showed that it could hold its own in the front line and at the Battle of the Somme the Commander-in-Chief, General Sir Douglas Haig, noted that it 'had advanced further and [taken] more prisoners than any division had done in one day'. The enemy, however, was not the only opposition with which the RND had to contend. The Army leaders, confounded by the Division's attachment to its naval heritage, tried forcibly to mould the sailors into a wholly military unit. That resulted in yet another victory for the Royal Naval Division.

The divisional badge (worn on the upper right arm)

Divisional shoulder titles

From 1916, this shoulder title was used at the RND training depots as a cap badge prior to joining a battalion.

Battalion cap badges

Anson Battalion.   Howe Battalion.   Hood Battalion.

Battalion cap badges

Drake Battalion.   Hawke Battalion.   Nelson Battalion.

Machine Gunner cap badge

Machine Gunner variation.

Machine Gunner variation.

Battalion shoulder titles

Drake Battalion.

Rating using a shoulder badge as a cap badge.

Anson Battalion.

Rating of the Howe Battalion using a section of goldwire cap-tally as a cap badge.

15 Royal Naval Air Service Ratings' Cap Badges

Chief Petty Officer from General Service.

Petty Officer from General Service.

A RNAS Petty Officer with General Service experience, c.1916. The vertical stripe on his left cuff is a 'Wound badge'.

Chief Petty Officer with solely RNAS service.

Petty Officers and junior ratings with solely RNAS service.

Petty Officer with just RNAS service, c.1916. (The exposed buttons at the collar are an affectation.)

A RNAS junior rating, c.1916.

16 Reserve Ratings' Cap Badges

THE ROYAL NAVAL RESERVE

The Royal Naval Reserve (RNR) was first recruited from merchant seamen in 1859 in response to a manpower shortage exposed by the Crimean War. During the nineteenth century, the highest rate that could be achieved was that of Able Seaman and Fireman. In 1905, Engine Room Artificers and Leading Seamen were allowed, leading to a full range of rates by the time of the outbreak of the First World War.

Trained Man 1873–1893.

Engine Room Artificer 1905–1915. Then as for Chief Petty Officer (Military Branch).

Chief Petty Officer (Military Branch) 1914–1923. Then as for Royal Naval Chief Petty Officers.

Chief Petty Officer (Civil Branch) 1914–1918. Then as for Military Branch.

Ratings in Class III uniforms 1914–1923.

Royal Naval Reserve, Trawler Section Engineman, c.1916.

THE ROYAL NAVAL VOLUNTEER RESERVE

Founded in 1903, the Royal Naval Volunteer Reserve (RNVR) provided an additional reserve for the Royal Navy. It was recruited from men with no professional sea-going experience yet, during both world wars, it provided a valuable and much-respected source of manpower. This was recognized in 1958 when the RNVR was absorbed into the RNR.

Chief Petty Officer (Military Branch) 1914–1923.

Chief Petty Officer (Military Branch) variation.

Chief Petty Officer (Civil Branch) 1914–1923.

Chief Petty Officer
(Civil Branch) variation.

Engine Room Artificer 1914.

Engine Room Artificer variation.

Engine Room Artificer 1915–1918
(then as for Military Branch).

Engine Room Artificer variant.

Ratings in Class III uniforms
1914–1923. Then as for Royal
Naval ratings in Class III uniforms.

Ratings in Class III
uniform variation.

Royal Naval Volunteer Reserve Engine Room
Artificer, c.1916 (purple background).

THE ROYAL NAVAL MOTOR BOAT RESERVE

The Royal Naval Motor Boat Reserve (RNMBR) was created in the early part of 1914 in response to the owners of small, fast craft wanting to play a part in any approaching conflict. Throughout the First World War, under the authority of the RNVR, the RNMBR patrolled harbours, docks, booms and anchorages for signs of enemy activity, including mines and submarines. After performing a valuable role in the war effort, the RNMBR was disbanded in 1918.

Chief Motor Boatman
1914–1916 (metal).

Motor Boatman
1914–1916 (metal).

Chief Motor Mechanic
1916–1918.

Motor Mechanic 1916–1918.
Motor Boatman 1916–1918.

THE ROYAL NAVAL RESERVE – TRAWLER SECTION (1910–1921)

Established in 1910, and with its first members joining the following year, the RNR(T) provided the Royal Navy with a minesweeping capability. Made up from men with experience in trawlers, it did valuable work throughout the First World War. In 1921, it was taken into the Royal Naval Reserve, only to re-emerge during the Second World War as the Royal Naval Patrol Service.

Skipper.

Deckhand or Stoker.

Engineman 1914.

Engineman 1914–1921.

Chief Motor Mechanic, c.1916 (purple background).

Chief Petty Officer Royal Naval Volunteer Reserve Anti-Aircraft Corps, c.1915. The moustache was permitted for wear by 'Hostilities Only' officers and ratings.

THE FISHERY RESERVE (1918–1921)

The Fishery Reserve was instituted in 1918 and consisted of trawlers and their crews who were available to the Admiralty for help with minesweeping after the First World War. It was disbanded in 1921.

Chief Skipper, Group Skipper, Skipper.

Second Hand, Royal Naval Reserve, Trawler Section, c.1915.

17 Shoulder Badges and Tabs

ROYAL NAVAL RATING'S SHOULDER BADGES AND TABS

With the introduction of woollen pullovers and a new pattern of foul-weather clothing, it was decided in 1970 that shoulder badges should be issued to ratings. At first, only Chief Petty Officers were allowed to wear the badges on the shoulder straps of the woollen pullover, while Petty Officers and Leading Hands were required to sew on a red-embroidered arm badge. When this proved to be impractical, a new range of shoulder badges was introduced in 1979, and the 1970 pattern was then limited to the foul-weather clothing. The fitting of shoulder straps to a wide range of tropical and working clothing, and the discontinuation of the red-embroidered arm badges, saw the introduction of gold-embroidered camouflage and desert-wear shoulder badges. When worn with desert and camouflage clothing, the shoulder badge can be worn as a tab on the front of the chest. With the newly formed Royal Naval Police Branch taking over from the Regulating Branch, shoulder badges specific to that branch were introduced.

1970 pattern

Fleet Chief Petty Officer (after 1979 for wear only with foul-weather clothing).

Chief Petty Officer (after 1979 for wear only with foul-weather clothing).

Petty Officer (for wear only with foul-weather clothing).

Leading rate (for wear only with foul-weather clothing).

1979 pattern

Fleet Chief Petty Officer 1979–1984. Warrant Officer 1984–2004.

Chief Petty Officer 1979–2004.

Petty Officer.

Leading rate.

1995 pattern

Warrant Officer.

Chief Petty Officer.

Petty Officer.

Leading rate.

2004 pattern

Warrant Officer 1st Class.

Warrant Officer 2nd Class.

Chief Petty Officer.

Petty Officer.

Leading rate.

Able rate and below.

For wear as tabs with camouflage clothing

Warrant Officer 1st Class.

Warrant Officer 2nd Class.

Chief Petty Officer.

Petty Officer.

Leading rate.

Able rate and below.

For wear with desert clothing

Warrant Officer 1st Class.

Warrant Officer 2nd Class.

Chief Petty Officer.

Petty Officer.

Leading Hand.

Able rate and below.

Royal Naval Police 2004–

Petty Officer.

Leading Hand.

Royal Naval Reserves (examples)

Royal Naval Reserve
Chief Petty Officer.

Royal Naval Reserve
Petty Officer.

Chief Petty Officer 1975.

Chief Petty Officer on attachment to the British Army 2006.

Chief Petty Officer in a shore combat zone 2006. His rate can be identified from the tab on his chest.

Able Rating 2010.

Petty Officer Royal Naval Police, 2010.

18 Collar/Tie Badges

The collar badge was introduced in 1970 for wear on either side of the shirt collar when a tie was being worn. This, however, caused too much damage to the shirt collar and, shortly after their introduction, the badges were ordered to be worn on the tie itself. The badges continued to be worn on the collars of open-neck tropical and working shirts until the widespread use of shoulder badges did away with the need for collar badges. The badges were officially phased out by 1989, but continued to be worn on ties many years later.

Fleet Chief Petty Officer 1970–1984.
Warrant Officer 1984–1989.

Chief Petty Officer.

Petty Officer.

Chief/Stoker c.1910.

Seaman Gunner Torpedo Man with the rate of Petty Officer 2nd Class c.1885.

19 Boys, Juniors, Boy Artificers, Artificer Apprentices and Apprentices

BOYS 1868–1956, JUNIORS 1956–

It was not at all unusual for 14- and 15-year-old boys to enter the Royal Navy during the latter part of the nineteenth century and the first half of the twentieth century. Even in the 1960s, 15-year-olds were regularly entering. Consequently, by the time such individuals were approaching the age of 18 (the time when a 'Man's' continuous service engagement began), it was quite possible that they would have two or more years' experience, even at sea. To take advantage of this experience, selected 'Boys' (1868–1954) and 'Juniors' (1954–) were given a temporary rate. This gave them an authority over other Boys and Juniors (although only those who were their training-ship peers) that was surrendered on being drafted elsewhere. The award of the temporary rate, however, remained on the individual's Service Record as a possible indicator of future leadership potential.

Instructor Boy 1898–1956, Junior Instructor 1956–

Instructor Boy 1898–1901.

Instructor Boy 1901–1922.

Instructor Boy 1922–1953.

Instructor Boy 1953–1956.
Junior Instructor 1956–.

Petty Officer Boys 1868–1956, Petty Officer Juniors 1956–

Chief Petty Officer Boy (1868–1901?). Speculative, but based upon photographic evidence.

Petty Officer Boy 1868–1878.

Petty Officer Boy 1878–1882.

Petty Officer Boy 1882–1901.

Boy Seamen preparing to receive cavalry c.1900. The boy next to the Warrant Officer appears to be wearing the obsolete Chief Petty Officer's arm badge (*see* insert). Although speculative, it is possible that he holds the rate of 'Chief Petty Officer Boy' as an additional rate to the recorded Petty Officer Boy and Leading Boy.

Others

Petty Officer Boy
1901–1953.

Petty Officer Boy
1953–1956. Petty Officer
Junior 1956–.

Leading Boy 1919–1956.
Leading Junior 1956–.

Advanced Class Boy
1917–1922.

Advanced Class Boy
1922–1956. 1st Class
Junior 1956–.

**BOY ARTIFICERS, ARTIFICER APPRENTICES,
AND APPRENTICES.**

With the spread of Trades Unionism throughout Britain, it was decided in 1903 that, rather than risk such ideas entering the Royal Navy via the fully trained Engine Room Artificers, it would be better to start an apprentice scheme that would train boys in their skills within the Service. As with the other branches of the Service, experienced Apprentices were selected and given authority over their Apprentice peers. When the individual was drafted, the rate was surrendered.

Boy Artificers 1906–1920, Artificer Apprentices 1920–1954, Apprentices 1954–2003

Petty Officer Boy Artificer 1906–1920 (left cuff only). Petty Officer Artificer Apprentice 1920–1954 (left cuff only). Petty Officer Apprentice 1954–2003 (left cuff only). Chief Petty Officer Apprentice (both cuffs) 1954–2003.

Red embroidered version
for No. 2 uniform.

Leading Apprentice
1954–2003 (left cuff only).

Petty Officer Boy, c.1885.

Leading Boy, c.1925.

20 Nuclear, Biological and Chemical Suit Badges, 1990–

When dressed in a Nuclear, Biological and Chemical (NBC) protection suit, complete with respirator (gas-mask), it is practically impossible to identify the wearer. Consequently, stick-on rate identification badges were introduced.

Warrrant Officer 1st Class.

Warrant Officer 2nd Class.

Chief Petty Officer.

Petty Officer.

Leading Hand.

21 Ratings' Buttons

Prior to the introduction of the Dress Regulations of 1857, which introduced a uniform for ratings, there was no approved policy regarding the buttons worn by ratings. The introduction of the new regulations in January of that year, however, saw, from 1860, the introduction of a rimless, black horn button for ratings' use. Certain ratings holding a rate equivalent to Chief Petty Officer were granted the use of the button then in use by officers below the rank of Flag Officer in 1868. Chief Petty Officers were, themselves, granted this privilege five years later. In 1890 new regulations stated that the rating's gilt button was to be of the same design as that of the officers, 'except that the crown and anchor is to be surrounded by a plain rim'. However, when the new uniform regulations were issued, in the following year, the illustration of the officer's button showed the button with a plain background replacing the lined background previously in use. This novel–and possibly unintended–arrangement was adopted for the officer's button, but ignored as far as the rating's button was concerned; the latter remained available only with the lined background. In the 1970s, the gilt button for ratings was replaced by an 'anodized' version.

1860–1890. Black horn button used by Engine Room Artificers, Schoolmasters, and Masters-at-Arms until 1868. Chief Petty Officers wore it until 1873, Petty Officers until 1890.

1868–1888. Officer's pattern gilt button used by Engine Room Artificers, Schoolmasters and Masters-at-Arms. Chief Petty Officers were granted this button in 1873.

1890–1901. All Chief Petty Officers.

Example of black horn button with rim, worn, in this case, between 1890 and 1901.

1901–1921. Royal Naval Reserve rating's button. It was restored for use between 1951 and 1953.

1901–1921. Royal Naval Volunteer Reserve rating's button. It was restored for use between 1951 and 1953.

1890–1901. Royal Naval Reserve rating's button.

1901–1953. Rating's button.

White plastic button for use with tropical, medical and catering uniform. This example was for use between 1901 and 1953.

1953–rating's button.

1953–1958 Royal Naval Reserve rating's button.

1953–1958 Royal Naval Volunteer Reserve rating's button.

Leading Hand with black horn buttoning jacket, c.1885.

A junior rating wearing an 1891 pattern jacket with black horn buttons. Normally, unless it was raining, the collar was worn outside the jacket.

22 The Women's Royal Naval Service (WRNS)

The WRNS were founded in November 1917, under the slogan of 'Free a Man for the Fleet'. Beginning with mainly domestic occupations, it was not long before the WRNS not only demonstrated the capability of handling a wider range of skills, but also served abroad. Nevertheless, the Treasury refused them the opportunity to wear gold lace, requiring them to wear royal blue cuff stripes, which had a tendency to fade to a lighter blue over time. Ratings were also given blue rate and branch badges.

After just nineteen months of existence, the end of the First World War also saw the end of the WRNS. With the outbreak of the Second World War, having made a lasting impression dur-

ing their first, short existence, the WRNS were re-constituted. They went on to provide a valuable service during the war, with more than 74,000 women serving in the years up to 1945. This time the Royal Navy recognized their continuing value and put the WRNS on a permanent footing in 1949, although they remained outside the Royal Navy as a separate organization until they were brought under the Naval Discipline Act, in 1977. This change in their status led the way to full integration into the Royal Navy in 1993, an action which saw the ending of the WRNS uniform and insignia, and the adoption of gold lace for officers and gold badges for ratings.

WOMEN'S ROYAL NAVAL SERVICE (WRNS) OFFICERS

Cap badges

1917–1919.

1939–1953.

War issue metal crown 1940–1945.

1953–1993.

Hat bands 1987–1983

Chief Commandant.   Commandant, Superintendent, Chief Officer.

Cuff stripes 1917–1919
(Note: The 'Principles' and Quarters Supervisor adopted the 'diamond' late 1918)

Director.   Deputy Director.   Assistant Director.   Deputy Assistant Director.

Senior WRNS officers 1917.

Divisional Director.

Deputy Divisional Director.

Principal 1917–1918.

Deputy Principal 1917–1918.

Assistant Principal
1917–1918.

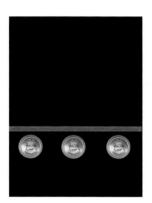

Quarters Supervisor
1917–1918.

Director 1958.

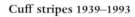

Cuff stripes 1939–1993

Director 1939–1946, Com-
mandant 1940–1951, Chief
Commandant 1951–1993.

Director 1946–1951,
Commandant 1951–1993.

Deputy Director
1939–1940, Superintendent
1940–1993.

Superintendent 1939–1940,
Chief Officer 1940–1993.

Chief Officer 1939–1940,
First Officer 1940–1993.

First Officer 1939–1940,
Second Officer 1940–1993.

Second Officer 1939–1940,
Third Officer 1940–1993.

Accountant or Supply
Branch 1939–1956.

Director 1917.

Divisional Director 1918.

Principal 1918.

Medical Superintendent 1939–1940.
(After 1940 Medical and Dental
Officers wore the gold stripes of
their Royal Naval equivalents.)

Women's Royal Naval Service
Reserve Officer 1951–1993.

An example of the WRNS cuff stripes
as illustrated in the 1966 Uniform
Regulations. This version was worn by
The Women's Royal Indian Naval
Service (WRINS), never by the WRNS.

Senior WRNS officers 1945.

WOMEN'S ROYAL NAVAL SERVICE (WRNS) RATINGS

Cap badges

Fleet Chief Petty Officer
1970–1985, Warrant Officer
1985–1990.

Warrant Officer 1990–1993
(then as for Royal Navy).

Chief Section Leader
1917–1918 (gold wire anchor).

Chief Petty Officer 1939–1953.

Petty Officer 1939–1953.

An Assistant Principal checks a rating's gas mask c.1917.

Fleet Chief and Warrant Officer cuffs 1970–1993

**Chief Petty Officer
Wren's cuff 1939–**

Fleet Chief Petty Officer 1970–
1985 (badge on left cuff only).

Warrant Officer 1985–1993
(then as for Royal Navy).

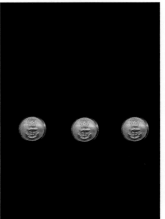

1953 pattern buttons.

1917–1919

**Petty Officer Wren arm badges 1939–1993
(then as for Royal Navy)**

Section Leader.

Leader.

1939–1953.

1953–1993.

Leading Wren arm badge 1939–1993 (then as for Royal Navy)

Chief Section Leaders c.1918.

Shoulder badges 1970–1993 (then as for Royal Navy)

Fleet Chief Petty Officer
1970–1985, Warrant
Officer 1985–1993.

Chief Petty Officer.

Petty Officer.

Leading rate.

Collar/Tie badges 1970–1989 then phased out on the introduction of shoulder badges

Fleet Chief Petty Officer
1970–1985, Warrant Officer
1985–1989.

Chief Petty Officer.

Petty Officer.

Accompanied by a Third and a First Officer, the Duchess of Kent, in the uniform of a Director,
talks to a Leading Wren, c.1943.

23 Royal Marines

The Royal Marines were founded upon infantrymen raised to serve at sea in 1664, and have retained their military-style organization since those days. The name 'Marines' was first applied in 1672 with the award of the distinction 'Royal' being granted in 1802. The 'Blue Marines' of the newly formed Royal Marine Artillery (RMA) were introduced in 1804 to serve alongside the 'Red Marines' of the Royal Marine Light Infantry (RMLI). The uniform worn by the Royal Marines reflected the style of the army uniform that was contemporaneous, with hats moving from tricorns to bicorns to shakos (black cylindrical hats with peaks), and then to helmets, which were first introduced in 1905. Caps ranged in design from the pillbox, the Glengarry and the peakless 'Broderick' of 1903 to the field service cap of 1897 and the blue beret of 1943. The green 'Commando' beret was introduced into the Royal Marines in 1960 and is worn only by those who have completed the Commando course. From the shako onwards, all required a badge to indicate the wearer's social position (officer or other rank), with arm, shoulder or cuff badges to indicate actual rank. The rank badges continued to follow the army tradition of crowns, stars ('pips') and stripes.

In 1923, the RMLI and the RMA were amalgamated in the face of threatened Treasury cuts, and reverted to the sole title 'Royal Marines' with the old army rank of 'Private' being replaced by 'Marine'. The blue uniform of the RMA was retained with the addition of the slashed 'mariner's cuff' and a red stripe down the trousers in remembrance of the red RMLI uniform. The 'Globe and Laurel' badge, first introduced during the time of King George IV, was adopted as the 'Corps' badge and used for wear on caps and berets. Originally, Sergeants and above wore a gilt version, with junior ranks wearing a badge of polished brass. Anodized badges were introduced for all ranks in 1958. A bronze version was worn in khaki service dress from the date of the merger, with a Bakelite version being produced for economy reasons during the Second World War. Since 1964, the bronze cap badge has been worn by all ranks in the field. From 1941, all ranks wore a red flash behind the badge on completion of basic training. With the introduction of the green beret, the red flash is worn on a blue beret only by Marines under training.

Royal Marine Officers (examples)
shako plates

Royal Marine Light Infantry 1856–1866.

Royal Marine Light Infantry 1866–1878.

Royal Marine Light Infantry 1866–1878 variant.

Helmet plates

Royal Marine Light Infantry 1878–1901.

Royal Marine Light Infantry 1878–1901 variant.

Royal Marine Artillery 1878–1905.

Royal Marine Light Infantry 1901–1905.

Royal Marines 1905–1953.

Royal Marines 1953–.

Other headgear

Busby badge and plume holder 1862–1878.

Glengarry badge 1870–1897.

Cap badges

Royal Marine Light Infantry 1880–1923.

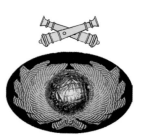

Royal Marine Artillery 1880–1923.

General Officers (example showing
pre-1953 crown).

Brigadiers and Colonels.

1923–1953.

1953–.

Cap peaks 1953–

General Officers.

Brigaders, Colonels, Lieutenant Colonels, Majors.

Gorget patches

General Officers.

Brigadiers and Colonels.

Royal Marine Light Infantry
Officer c.1895.

Collar badges

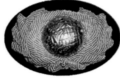

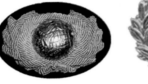

Pre-1923 dress uniform.

Blue uniform.

Mess jacket shoulder stripes

General Officers.

Brigadiers and Colonels.

Royal Marine Captain serving as a pilot with the
Royal Naval Air Service c.1915.

Shoulder straps

General.

Lieutenant General.

Major General.

Brigadier.

Colonel.

Lieutenant Colonel.

Major.

Captain.

Lieutenant.

Second Lieutenant.

Buttons

General Officers.

Brigadiers and Colonels.

Chin straps.

All other officers.

Cuff insignia 1914–1918

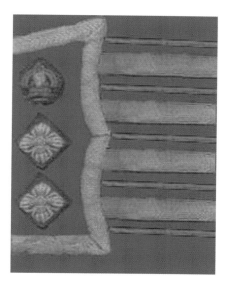

Colonel.

Lieutenant Colonel.

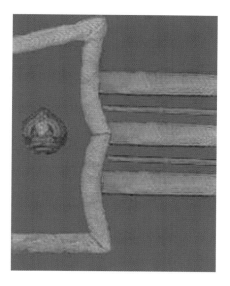

Major.

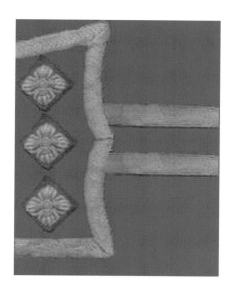

Captain.

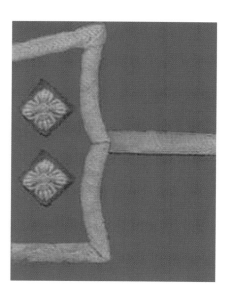

Lieutenant.

Second Lieutenant.

Royal Marine Warrant Officers and Other Ranks (examples)
Shako plates

Royal Marines 1854–1866.

Royal Marines Light Infantry
1866–1878.

Helmet plates

Royal Marines Light Infantry
1878–1901.

Royal Marines Light Infantry
1901–1905.

Royal Marine Light Infantry Bugler
wearing the 1870–1897 Glengarry badge.

Royal Marine Light Infantry Private c.1895.

Royal Marines 1905–1953.

Royal Marines 1953–.

Other headgear

Royal Marine Artillery Warrant Officer's busby badge and plume holder 1863–1878.

Royal Marine Artillery Other Ranks busby and plume holder 1863–1878.

Royal Marine Light Infantry Glengarry badge 1870–1897.

Royal Marine Light Infantry Private wearing the 1870–1897 Glengarry badge.

Royal Marine Artillery pillbox cap badges 1874–1892

Lance Sergeant.

Bombadier.

Lance Bombadier.

Private.

Cap badges

Royal Marine Light Infantry 1892–1923.

Sergeant Royal Marine Artillery 1892–1923.

Other Ranks Royal Marine Artillery 1892–1923.

Royal Marines Labour Corps 1916–1919.

Warrant Officer Royal Marines 1923–1953.

Other Ranks Royal Marines 1923–1953.

Warrant Officer 1st Class 2004–.

Warrant Officer 1953–2004, Warrant Officer 2nd Class 2004–.

Other Ranks 1953–.

Other Ranks, bronze version 1953–.

Warrant Officer's cuff badges (2007)

Warrant Officer 1st Class.

Warrant Officer 2nd Class.

Royal Marine c.1930. The chevrons above his left cuff are good conduct badges.

Non-commissioned Officer's rank stripe (Blue Uniform) 1953–

Colour Sergeant.

Sergeant.

Corporal.

Sergeants on the Staff (worn on the right cuff)

Lance-Corporal.

Colour Sergeant's stripes for lovat uniform 1963–.

Sergeant mess dress

Sergeant Armourer (obsolete).

Provost Sergeant.

Hospital Sergeant in charge of the Infirmary (obsolete).

Royal Marine Light Infantry Colour Sergeant badges. Worn on the right arm, they were worn above three stripes from 1881

1830–1868.

1868–1881.

1881–1901.

1901–1923.

Royal Marine Artillery Colour Sergeant's badges. worn on the right arm, they were worn above three stripes from 1881

1862–1868.

1868–1901.

1901–1923.

Royal Marine Colour Sergeant's badges. Worn on the right arm, they were worn on the right arm of the blue uniform above three stripes

1923–1953.

1953–.

Collar badges

Warrant Officer 1st Class 2004–.   Other ranks.

Button

RMA 1901–1923.   1923–1953.   1953–(bronze).   1953–(Staybright).

Royal Marine Artillery Lance Bombardier
wearing the 1874–1892 pillbox cap badge.

Royal Marine Sergeant c.1925.

Royal Marine c.1928.

The Royal Marines Band (examples only)
It should be noted that, in general, rank insignia is identical to that of the Royal Marines.

Officers' helmet plates

Royal Marines Artillery Band
Master's busby badge 1860–1878.

Chatham Royal Marines Light
Infantry Band 1905–1950.

Royal Marines Band, Portsmouth Group
1955–1972. Band of Commander-in-Chief,
Naval Home Command 1972–. Band of
Her Majesty's Royal Marines, Portsmouth.

Warrant Officers and Other Ranks helmet plates

Royal Marines Band, Plymouth Division
1953–. Band of Her Majesty's Royal Marines Commando Training Centre.

Chatham Royal Marines Light Infantry
Band 1905–1923. Royal Marines Band
Chatham Division 1923–1950.

Plymouth Royal Marines Light Infantry
1920–1923. Royal Marines Band, Plymouth
Division 1923–1953.

Royal Marines Band, Plymouth Division 1953–. Band of Her
Majesty's Royal Marine Commando Training Centre.

Royal Marines Band, Portsmouth Group 1955–1972. Band of
Commander-in-Chief Naval Home Command. Band of Her
Majesty's Royal Marines Portsmouth.

Royal Naval School of Music and bands without specific cap badges 1903–1950
Cap badges

Bandmaster.

Bandsman.

Early Bandsman split variety.

Cap badges of other bands

Royal Marines Band, Portsmouth 1903–1911.

Royal Marines Band, Portsmouth 1911–1923. Band of the
Royal Marines, Portsmouth Division 1923–1947. Royal Marines
Band, Portsmouth Group. 1947–1955.

Royal Marines Band, Portsmouth Group, 1955–1972. Band of
Commander-in-Chief, Naval. Home Command, 1972–1997.
Band of HM Royal Marines, Portsmouth 1997–.

Chatham Royal Marines Light Infantry Band
1902–1923.

Plymouth Royal Marine Light Infantry Band 1902–1911.

Plymouth Royal Marines Light Infantry Band 1911–1923.

Royal Marine Band, Chatham 1923–1950.

Band of the Royal Marines, Plymouth 1923–1953.

Royal Marines Band, Plymouth 1953–. Band of Her Majesty's Commando Training Centre.

Collar badges

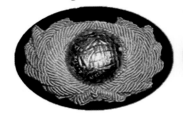

Officer's dress uniform 1923–.

Bandmaster, brass, blue uniform, 1903–1950.

Bandsman, brass, blue uniform, 1903–1950.

Bandsman, embroidered cotton, dress uniform, 1904–1950.

Drum Major c.1860.

Band Corporals, Musicians, embroidered cotton, c.1950–.

Sergeants, gold thread, 1950–.

Other badges

Bandmaster 1953–1968 (worn on right cuff).

Warrant Officer 2nd Class, Bandmaster.

Other Bandsmen.

Royal Marine Light Infantry Drum Major, c.1860. (Worn on both upper arms.)

Drum Major (worn on lower right arm).

Bugle Major (worn on lower right arm).

24 Queen Alexandra's Royal Naval Nursing Service (QARNNS)

Prior to 1884, Royal Naval hospitals were staffed in part by women who were the wives or associates of the patients, and in part by women of doubtful reputation. In the latter years of the century, the enrolment of trained nurses to assist the surgeons proved to be such a success that, in 1902, Queen Alexandra began to take an interest, becoming the patron of an organization that soon became known as the 'QARNNS'. Indeed, it is said that she became so closely involved that she designed the QARNNS badge with its crossed 'As' (sometimes inter-twined, sometimes overlaying each other) wrapped around a gold anchor.

The QARNNS were assisted at ward level by male Sick Berth Stewards (later 'Sick Berth Attendants', or SBAs). With the outbreak of the First World War, the SBAs were required for sea duties and were replaced by Volunteer Aid Detachment women

Queen Alexandra's Royal Naval Nursing Service (QARNNS) sisters and officers

Cap badge

1953–.

Hat bands 1982–

Superintending Nursing Officer 1982–1995, Lieutenant Commander 1995–.

Principal Nursing Officer 1982–1995, Chief Nursing Officer 1982–1995, Captain, Commander 1995–.

Matron-in-Chief 1982–1995, Commodore 1995–.

Cape badge

Head Sister-in-Chief 1927–1940, Matron-in-Chief 1940–1949.

Matron-in-Chief on appointment as Honorary Nursing Sister to the King 1949–1953.

Principal-Matron 1940–1953.

Head Sister 1902–1936, Matron 1936–1953.

Superintending Sister 1911–1953.

Senior Sister 1940–1953.

Sister 1902–1953.

Matron-in-Chief 1953–1995 (additionally, Director of Nursing Services 1982–1995).

(VADs), who were either untrained, or had just the rudiments of medical knowledge from the Red Cross or St John's Ambulance Brigade. Other assistance came from the QARNNS Reserves, which had been formed in 1910. The same arrangement continued throughout the Second World War. In 1949, Women's Royal Naval Service (WRNS) SBAs were introduced, only to be replaced, ten years later, by QARNNS Naval Nursing Auxiliaries (NANAs), who were to be trained at a newly created Royal Naval School of Nursing. Male nursing specialists known as 'Medical Technicians' were introduced in 1965–along with 'Naval Nurses' replacing the NANAs–and, in 1982, the QARNNS

was re-formed to allow males to enter the Service as equivalents of the Nursing Sisters. Consequently, the title of 'Sister' was replaced by 'Nursing Officer'. At the same time, Naval Nurses were put in to naval rating's uniform with appropriate marks of distinction, but continued to wear the QARNNS Nurses' cap badge.

Placed under the Naval Discipline Act in 1977, the QARNNS were fully integrated into the Royal Navy in 1995, with the Nursing Officers adopting the gold lace cuff stripes of naval officers, and senior rating nurses wearing a special QARNNS version of the Royal Navy cap badges.

Matron-in-Chief in rank of Principal Nursing Officer 1982–1995.

Principal Matron 1953–1982, Principal Nursing Officer 1982–1995.

Matron 1953–1982, Chief Nursing Officer 1982–1995.

Superintending Sister 1953–1982, Superintending Nursing Officer 1982–1995.

Senior Sister 1953–1982, Senior Nursing Officer 1982–1995.

Sister 1953–1982, Nursing Officer 1982–1995.

Captain 1995–.

Commander 1995–.

Lieutenant Commander 1995–.

Lieutenant 1995–.

Sub-Lieutenant 1995–.

Capes (badges shown only for illustration)

Matron-in-Chief 1953–1995, Commodore 1995–.

Head Sister 1902–1936, Superintending Nursing Sister 1911–1982, Matron 1939–1953, Principal Matron 1953–1982, Matron-in-Chief in rank of Principal Nursing Officer 1982–1995, Principal Nursing Officer 1982–1995, Matron 1953–1982, Chief Nursing Officer 1982–1995, Superintending Nursing Officer 1982–1995, Captain, Commander 1995–.

Officer's cuff (example)

Lieutenant Commander 1995–, badge worn on both cuffs.

Superintending Nursing Sister 1911–1982, Superintending Nursing Officer 1982–1995, Lieutenant Commander 1995–.

Nursing Sister 1902–1982, Senior Nursing Sister 1940–1982, Senior Nursing Officer 1982–1995, Nursing Officer 1982–1995, Sub-Lieutenant 1995–.

QARNNS Sisters 1918.

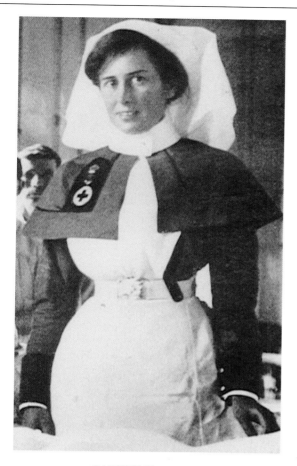

QARNNS Sister 1914.

Shoulder badges (examples)

1953–1995.   1995–.

Queen Alexandra's Royal Nursing Service Reserves (founded 1910)

Cape badges (examples). Note: Gold wire replaced with silver

Superintending Sister.   Sister.

Belt buckle

1902–1953. From 1953 the St Edward (Queen's) crown was used.

QARNNS Sisters c.1902.

QARNNS Sister c.1910.

Queen Alexandra's Royal Naval Nursing Service– Nursing Auxiliaries and Nurses
Cap badges

Head Naval Nursing Auxiliary 1960–1965, Assistant Head Naval Auxiliary 1960–1965, Naval Nursing Auxiliary 1960–1965, Head Naval Nurse 1965–1995, Assistant Head Naval Nurse 1965–1995, Naval Nurse 1965–1995.

Warrant Officer 1995–2004, Warrant Officers 1st and 2nd Class 2004–.

Chief Petty Officer 1995–.

Petty Officer 1995–.

Cuff Ranks 1960–1982. Red braid–left cuff only. (Also worn on dresses below left shoulder)

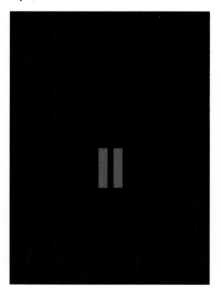

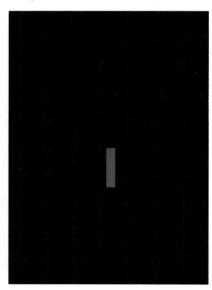

Head Naval Nursing Auxiliary 1960–1965, Head Naval Nurse 1965–1982.

Assistant Head Naval Nursing Auxiliary 1960–1965, Assistant Head Naval Nurse 1965–1982.

Senior Naval Nursing Auxiliary 1960–1965, Senior Naval Nurse 1965–1982.

Cuffs 1982–

Warrant Officer 1982–1986
(badge on left cuff only).

Warrant Officer 1986–1995
(originally on left cuff only, but later
extended to both cuffs).

Warrant Officer 1995–2004,
Warrant Officer 1st Class 2004–.

Warrant Officer 2nd Class 2004–.

Chief Petty Officer 1982–.

Blue Dress 1982–

Petty Officer.

Leading rate.

QARNNS Leading Nurse in Ward Dress 1989.

Working dress 1989–2006 (superseded by Royal Naval shoulder badges)

Tie Badges–1982 until phased out by 1989 with the widespread adoption of shoulder badges

Petty Officer.

Leading rate.

Warrant Officer.

Chief Petty Officer.

Petty Officer.

Shoulder badges 1989–2006 (female members of QARNNS from 1989 only). Royal Navy shoulder badges were then adopted

Warrant Officer 1982–1990.

Warrant Officer 1990–2004, Warrant Officer 1st Class 2004–.

Warrant Officer 2nd Class 2004–.

Chief Petty Officer.

Petty Officer.

Leading rate.

Belt buckle

Belts (similarly coloured shoulder badges are worn by trainee male nurses)

Registered General Nurse.

Enrolled Nurse (General).

Third Year trainee.

Second Year trainee.

First Year trainee.

25 The Royal Naval Mine Watching Service (RNMWS)

The Royal Naval Mine Watching Service (RNMWS) was established in 1952 as a force of volunteers who would observe the fall of mines from enemy aircraft, noting the position of the mines as they entered harbour waters. With mine watchers observing from several positions, the observations were cross-referenced, and the positions of the mines reported to the mine-clearance authorities. By the early 1960s, the RNMWS became involved with convoy assembly duties and, in 1963, had its title changed to the Royal Naval Auxiliary Service.

Royal Naval Mine Watching Service 1952–1963

Beret badge

Officers' shoulder badges (silver lace)

    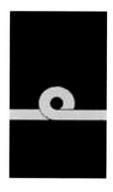

Command Naval Mine Watching Officer.

Area Naval Mine Watching Officer.

Port Naval Mine Watching Officer.

Senior Section Naval Mine Watching Officer.

Section Naval Mine Watching Officer.

Rate badges

Chief Naval Mine Watcher.

Leading Naval Mine Watcher.

26 The Royal Naval Auxiliary Service (RNXS)

With the disbandment of the Royal Naval Mine Watching Service (RNMWS) in 1963, its volunteers joined with volunteers who had served with the Admiralty Ferry Service (responsible during wartime for the transfer of small craft between ports) to create the Royal Naval Auxiliary Service (RNXS). The role of the new organization was to use its own dedicated small vessels to organize assembled merchant ships into convoys. In the case of a nuclear threat, the RNXS was to escort merchant ships out of port to be assembled at safe anchorages. Although there were numerous women members of the RNXS, all were known by the title 'Auxiliaryman'. The RNXS was disbanded as a cost-saving measure in 1994.

Royal Naval Auxiliary Service 1963–1994

Officers' beret badge 1977–1994.

Officers' shoulder badges 1963–1984 (silver wire)

Command Naval Auxiliary Officer.

Area Naval Auxiliary Officer.

Port Naval Auxiliary Officer.

Senior Section Naval Auxiliary Officer.

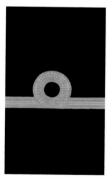

Section Naval Auxiliary Officer.

RNXS officers' cuff stripes 1984–1994

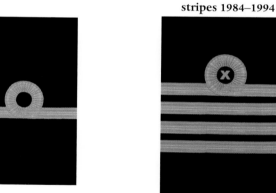

Auxiliary Captain.

Auxiliary Commander.

Auxiliary Lieutenant Commander.

Auxiliary Lieutenant.

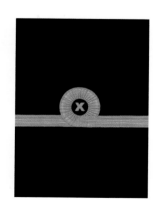

Auxiliary Officer.

RNXS female officers' cuff stripes 1984–1994

Auxiliary Captain.

Auxiliary Commander.

Auxiliary Lieutenant-Commander.

Auxiliary Lieutenant.

Officers' shoulder badges (samples)

Auxiliary Officer.

Auxiliary Lieutenant-Commander.

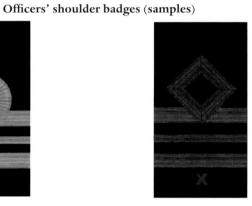

Auxiliary Lieutenant (female).

Rate badges 1984–1994

Chief Auxiliaryman (cuff buttons as for Chief Petty Officer, Royal Navy).

Leading Auxiliaryman.

Ratings' beret badge 1963–1994

Ratings' shoulder badges 1984–1994

Chief Auxiliaryman.

Leading Auxiliaryman.

27 British Merchant Navy, Post-1918

Just over two months before the end of the First World War, the Privy Council, with the approval of King George V, authorized the introduction of the first nationally agreed uniform–including insignia indicating rank and rate–for the Merchant Navy. Prior to the introduction, each company could wear whatever uniform it chose, or none at all. A few copied the Royal Navy with curls on the officers' cuff stripes, and with cap badges that closely followed the Royal Naval version. Under the new regulations, a company's employees could continue to wear the company cap badge in preference to the new version and, in time, several companies reverted to adopting their own style of officers' cuff stripes. The Merchant Navy has been included in this work, not just because it has been a prime source of Royal Naval Reserve officers, but because of the service it has rendered to its country for centuries. Since the introduction of an official uniform the Merchant Navy has been closely involved with the Royal Navy in the use of Catapult Aircraft Merchantmen (CAM ships), Defensively Equipped Merchant Ships (DEMS), Merchant Aircraft Carriers (MACs), and as transports–notably during the Falklands Conflict. The following illustrations represent the official 1918 version with examples of variations at the end.

Cap badges

Officers.

Ratings.

Officer's cuff stripes

Certificated Master.

Second Master.

Certificated Chief Officer.

First Officer.

Certificated Second Officer.

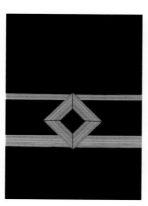

Junior Second Officer.

Certificated Third and Junior Certificated Officer.

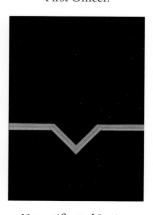

Uncertificated Junior Officer.

Certificated Chief Engineer.

Second Chief Engineer.

Certificated Second Chief and Chief
Refrigerating Engineer.

Junior Second Engineer.

Certificated Third Engineer and
Second Refrigerating Officer.

Junior Third Engineer.

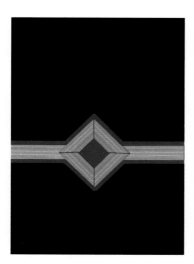

Certificated Fourth and
Junior Engineer.

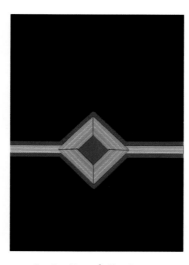

Junior Fourth Engineer.

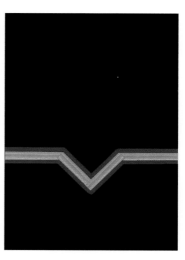

Uncertificated Junior Engineer
Refrigerating Engineer, Boilermaker
and Electrician.

Ship's Surgeon.

Assistant Ship's Surgeon.

Senior Purser where three or more are carried.

Purser.

Assistant Purser.

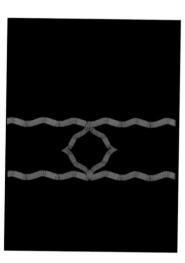

First Wireless Operator.

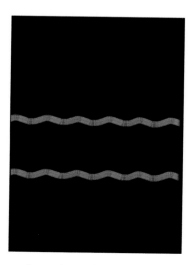

Second Wireless Operator.

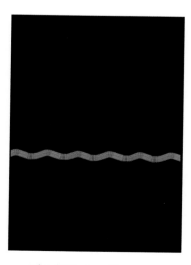

Third Wireless Operator.

Cadet or Apprentice.

Officer's shoulder straps (example)

Certificated Master.

Ratings' insignia
Cuff insignia (worn on both cuffs)

Chief Steward on passenger vessels.

Assistant Chief Steward.

Steward.

Assistant Steward.

Steward on Cargo Vessels.

Arm badges (worn on the left arm)

Boatswain.

Boatswain's Mate.

Quartermaster.

Quartermaster's Mate.

Cook.

Buttons

Officers.

Boatswains, Carpenters, Quartermasters, and equivalent Petty Officers. Junior ratings wore black horn buttons.

Stewards on cargo vessels (silver metal).

Examples of officers' cuff stripe variation

Mufti badge (authorized in 1940 for wear with civilian clothing to indicate that the wearer was engaged in vital war service)

Caledonian MacBrayne Line.

Cunard Line.

28 Maritime Volunteer Service

The Maritime Volunteer Service (MVS) was founded in 1994 with the aim of providing training for volunteers with an interest in maritime affairs and in learning maritime skills. It is an entirely self-funding organization that provides highly trained volunteers for maritime authorities at nautical events or emergencies.

Officers

Officer's cap badge.

Officer's Shoulder Badges (worn on each shoulder)

Chief Staff Officer.

Area Staff Officer,
Honorary Treasurer,
Honorary Secretary.

Regional Volunteer Officer.

Deputy Regional Volunteer
Officer.

Volunteer Officer.

Volunteer Officer (Engineer).

Other Grades

Other Grades beret badge.

Other Grades' Shoulder Badges (worn on each shoulder)

Chief Volunteer.

Petty Officer Volunteer.

Leading Volunteer.

Able Volunteer.

Volunteer.

Probationary Volunteer.

29 The Sea Cadets

The Sea Cadets can trace their origins back to the end of the Crimean War when steps were taken in 1856 to look after the orphans of naval men who had died during the conflict. Given public support by Queen Victoria in 1899, the charity took the name 'The Navy League Sea Cadet Corps' in 1919. This became 'The Sea Cadet Corps' (SCC) in 1942 with King George VI as the Corps Admiral. A Marine Cadet section was created in 1955 and, in 1980, the Girl's Naval Training Corps (formed in 1942) merged with the Sea Cadets. In 2004, the Marine Society (founded 1756) merged with the Sea Cadets to become the United Kingdom's largest maritime charity. The Marine Cadets were granted royal approval in 2010 to be renamed as the 'Royal Marines Cadets'. All officers hold their rank in the Royal Naval Reserve (RNR) or the Royal Marines Reserve (RMR). The cap badges and buttons of officers and instructor senior ratings remain as for those of the Royal Navy.

Sea Cadet Officers

Commander (SCC) RNR.

Lieutenant Commander (SCC) RNR.

Lieutenant (SCC) RNR.

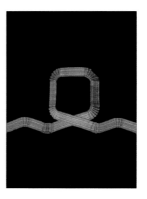

Sub Lieutenant (SCC) RNR.

Ratings

Midshipman (SCC) RNR.

Warrant Officer (SCC) (both cuffs).

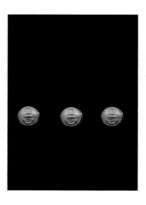

Chief Petty Officer (SCC) (both cuffs).

Petty Officer (SCC).

Probationary Petty Officer (SCC).

Petty Officer Cadet.

Leading Cadet.

Able Cadet.

Ratings

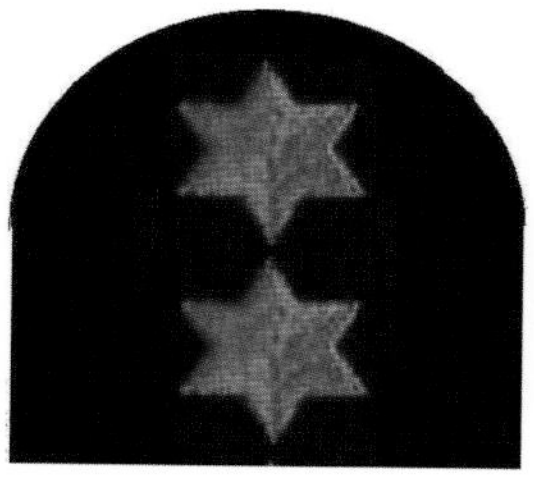

Ordinary Cadet.

Cadet.

Junior Section Ratings (aged 10–12)

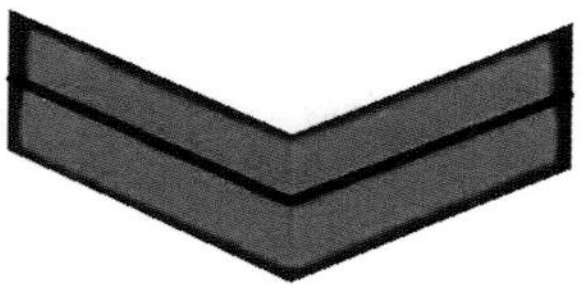

Leading Junior.

Junior First Class.

Royal Marine Cadet Officers

Major (SCC) RMR.

Captain (SCC) RMR.

Lieutenant (SCC) RMR.

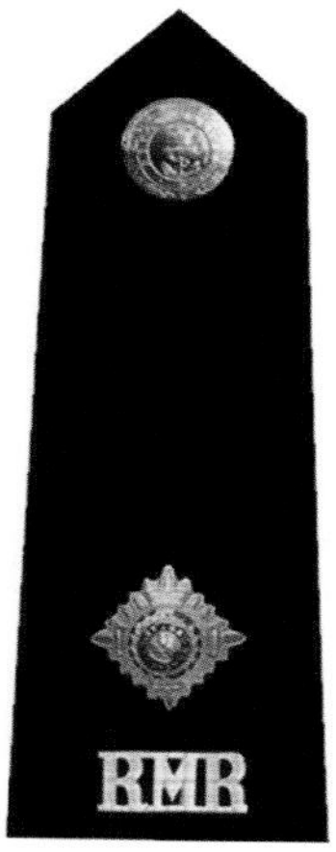

Second Lieutenant (SCC) RMR.

Royal Marine Cadet other ranks, for wear with blue uniform

Colour Sergeant (SCC).

Sergeant (SCC).

Corporal (SCC).

Lance Corporal (SCC).

For wear with camouflage uniform

Colour Sergeant (SCC).

Sergeant (SCC).

Probationary Sergeant (SCC).

Cadet Corporal (SCC).

Lance Corporal (SCC).

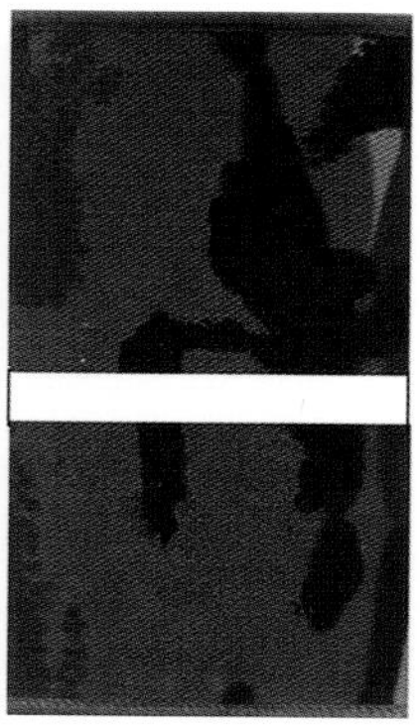

Cadet 1st Class (SCC).

30 Miscellaneous, Associated, Derivatives, Unauthorized and Unknown

Since the first introduction of the Royal Navy's modern uniform in 1856, both its design and associated insignia have been widely copied, not just in Great Britain and its former Dominions and Colonies, but throughout the entire world. The officer's cuff lace, gilt buttons and cap badge have found many echoes in foreign navies, both armed and merchant. A similar broad assumption of style has also been followed in the case of ratings. In this section, the aim is to keep generally within the British Isles, where there is a wealth of nautical association that has followed the insignia lead of the Royal Navy. Amongst the photographs may be seen something that occasionally causes difficulty for researchers: the incorrect use of insignia. Although the main reason behind this is probably an attempt to impress a young lady, the urge to over-decorate amongst, for example, the Royal Naval Air Service, can lead to confusion for a later generation. The same problems apply with unauthorized badges that have been locally produced.

Royal Dockyard Battalion shako plates 1847–1857

Dockyard Battalion button

Officers.

Other ranks.

Admiralty Barge Master 1890 (silver-gilt). The Admiralty maintained five barges for use on State occasions

Royal Naval Transport Service

Pre-1920 Royal Naval Transport officer. Some variants have the word 'TRANSPORT' above the anchor with no additional lettering.

Post 1920 HM Transport Petty Officer.

Unknown possibly early twentieth century Admiralty Messenger

Royal National Lifeboat Institution (shown with pre-1953 crowns)

Coxswain (some examples have a silver anchor).

Mechanic.

Other ratings.

HMS *Hamadryad*, Hospital Ship 1866–1905 (silver thread)

Naval Hospital Attendants

Volunteer Aid Detachments working in Royal Naval Hospitals

Senior Naval Hospital Attendant 1922–1939 (silver thread).

Naval Hospital Attendant 1922–1939.

1914–1918, 1939–1945.

Cable-Laying ships

Pre-1953 Cable-Laying Ship's officer.

Post-1953 Cable-Laying Ship's officer.

River Emergency Service 1939–1945

Officer (yellow thread).

Rating (yellow thread).

Rating variant (yellow thread).

Navy, Army, Air Force Institute (when at Sea)

NAAFI Canteen Manager
1939–1945.

NAAFI Canteen Assistant
1939–1945.

NAAFI Canteen Manager
1953–.

NAAFI Canteen Assistant 1953–.

Scottish Sea Fisheries

Possible Electrician's unofficial cap badge (pre-1920)

Possibly a pre-1920 Electrician attempting to copy the example of an Engine Room Artificer's purple velvet background by providing a green velvet background (green remains the colour associated with those maintaining electrical equipment in the Royal Navy).

Queen's Harbour Master

Cap badge.

Coastguard

Officer

Coastguard.

Customs and Excise

Cap badge.

Beret badge (brass).

**Civilian members of the
Admiralty Board 1953–**

**Civilian Admiralty (or,
later, Ministry of Defence
(Navy)) employee**

Cap badge.

Cap badge.

**'Mufti' badges (not strictly rank or rate badges but often mistaken for uniform insignia).
Worn on the lapel of a civilian jacket**

RNVR Anti-Aircraft Corps 1914–1916.
Based at Dover, Sheffield, London, and
with mobile corps in Kent and East Anglia.

Royal Naval Motor Boat Reserve
1914–1918.

RNAS Anti-Aircraft Corps 1914–1916. Defended
RNAS bases in France and the Aegean.
Sometimes found made of brass.

Admiralty War Service badge. Worn by civilians
working on vital shipbuilding projects.

Royal Naval Mine Watching Service.

Royal Naval Auxiliary Service.

Royal Naval Armoured Car Squadron Ratings' collar badge, worn in pairs. Frequently referred to as a cap badge

ROYAL FLEET AUXILIARY

Royal Fleet Auxiliary Officers' cap badges

Officer 1905–1920.

Officer 1920–1953.

Officer 1953–.

Officers of the White Star Line wearing uniforms almost indistinguishable from those of Royal Naval officers – only the cap badges and buttons are different. The officer on the right is Captain Edward Smith who went down with the *Titanic*. He is wearing the Reserve Decoration, awarded for his service with the Royal Naval Reserve.

Royal Fleet Auxiliary Officers' cuff stripes (Deck Officers shown)

Commodore.

Captain.

Chief Officer.

First Officer.

Royal Auxiliary Fleet Officers' cuff stripe branch colours

Second Officer.

Third Officer.

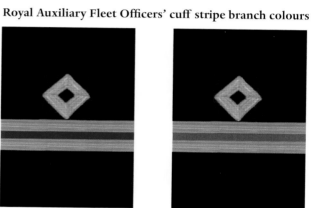

Engineering.

Surgeon.

Supply.

Communications.

System Engineering.

Royal Fleet Ratings' cap and beret badges

Junior Rating's beret badge 1953–.

Chief Petty Officer 1953–.

Petty Officer 1953–.

Admiralty Civilian Police 1922–1949

**Royal Marine Police (civilians employed as police officers to guard Royal Marine Barracks and other establishments) 1923–1949.
Royal Marine Police Special Reserve 1939–1949**

Admiralty Constabulary (civilian police officers employed to guard naval dockyards and establishments) 1949–1971

Cap badge.

Cap badge.

Cap badge.

Dockyard Police button 1945–1953 (silver domed).

Dockyard Police button 1953– (silver domed).

Colonial Dockyard Police (white metal)

A Sick Berth Steward (c.1910) who is wearing his three 'Good Conduct' stripes ('badges') on the wrong arm.

Late 19th century.

1901–1953.

Naval Schools

Royal Maritime Auxiliary Service 1976–

Greenwich Royal Naval School for Boys. Petty Officer Boy 1905–1933. (Worn on right arm.)

Merchant Navy Training Ship Worcester. Officer's cap badge.

Officer's cap badge.

Unofficial badges 1914–1918

Unauthorized, probably privately purchased, gold-plated version of the bronze officer's cap badge for wear ashore with khaki uniform.

Unauthorized, probably privately purchased, continental silver version of the Chief Petty Officer's bronze cap badge for wear with khaki uniform.

Unauthorized Royal Naval Air Service airship crews badge.

A Royal Naval Air Service Petty Officer Mechanic (c.1915) who has awarded himself an unauthorized matched pair of embroidered eagles for wear on his collar. The buttons showing in the collar cleft were a popular (but, again, unauthorized) affectation of the time.

St John Ambulance Brigade Auxiliary Sick Berth Reserve 1903–1949

Volunteers from the Brigade were sent to complete seven days' training in a Royal Naval hospital followed by another seven days at sea. Generally, they continued to wear the Brigade's uniform when serving at sea, but many opted to wear the uniform of the Royal Navy's Sick Berth (laters 'Sick Bay') ratings. These volunteers provided a valuable service throughout the First and Second World Wars.

Upper Thames Patrol

The Upper Thames Patrol was a Home Guard unit during the Second World War. In small boats, manned by soldiers, they were responsible for checking the Thames bridges for attempts of sabotage or, alternatively, for destroying the bridges to delay any invader. Their headquarters were frequently in public houses, which gave rise to the suggestion that the letters 'UTP' stood for 'Upstream To Pub.'

A Royal Naval Air Service Petty Officer Despatch Rider (c.1915) wearing a Chief Petty Officer's cap badge, and an altered Telegraphist's wings above the letters 'RNAS' on his collar. The badge of a Despatch Rider was a spoked, winged wheel and would have been worn on the right arm.

Services Rendered badge

During the First World War, this badge was issued to servicemen who had been injured during active service and invalided out of the armed forces, or were recovering from injuries prior to returning to active service. Worn on the lapel of civilian clothing, the badge help fend off women eager to hand out white feathers to men not wearing uniform on the assumption that such men were shirking their duty. Each badge was numbered, with those issued to men of the Royal Navy having the number preceded by the letters 'RN'.